Manage Your Customers, Manage Your Product

Techniques For Product Managers To Better Understand What Their Customers Really Want

"Practical, proven examples of how to get the customer insights that are necessary in order to have a successful product"

Dr. Jim Anderson

Published by:
Blue Elephant Consulting
Tampa, Florida

Printed in the United States of America

Library of Congress Control Number: 2017933692

ISBN-13: 978-1543043051
ISBN-10: 1543043054

Warning – Disclaimer

The purpose of this book is to educate and entertain. This book does not promise or guarantee that anyone following the ideas, tips, suggestions, techniques or strategies will be successful. The author, publisher and distributor(s) shall have neither liability nor responsibility to anyone with respect to any loss or damage caused, or alleged to be caused, directly or indirectly by the information contained in this book.

<u>Recent Books By</u>
<u>The Author</u>

<u>Product Management</u>

- Managing Your Product Manager Career: How Product Managers Can Find And Succeed In The Right Job

- How Product Managers Can Sell More Of Their Product: Tips & Techniques For Product Managers To Better Understand How To Sell Their Product

<u>Public Speaking</u>

- Creating Speeches That Work: How To Create A Speech That Will Make Your Message Be Remembered Forever!

- How To Organize A Speech In Order To Make Your Point: How to put together a speech that will capture and hold your audience's attention

<u>CIO Skills</u>

- How CIOs Can Bring Business And IT Together: How CIOs Can Use Their Technical Skills To Help Their Company Solve Real-World Business Problems

- New IT Technology Issues Facing CIOs: How CIOs Can Stay On Top Of The Changes In The Technology That

Powers The Company

IT Manager Skills

- How IT Managers Can Use New Technology To Meet Today's IT Challenges: Technologies That IT Managers Can Use In Order to Make Their Teams More Productive

- How To Build High Performance IT Teams: Tips And Techniques That IT Managers Can Use In Order To Develop Productive Teams

Negotiating

- The Art Of Packaging A Negotiation: How To Develop The Skill Of Assembling Potential Trades In Order To Get The Best Possible Outcome

- Getting What You Want In A Negotiation By Learning How To Signal: How To Develop The Skill Of Effective Signaling In A Negotiation In Order To Get The Best Possible Outcome

Miscellaneous

- How To Heal A Broken Leg – Fast!: Understanding how to deal with a broken leg in order to start walking again quickly

- How Software Defined Networking (SDN) Is Going To Change Your World Forever: The Revolution In Network Design And How It Affects

Note: See a complete list of books by Dr. Jim Anderson at the back of this book.

Acknowledgements

Any book like this one is the result of years of real-world work experience. In my over 25 years of working for 7 different firms, I have met countless fantastic people and I've been mentored by some truly exceptional ones. Although I've probably forgotten some of the people who made me the person that I am today, here is my attempt to finally give them the recognition that they so truly deserve:

- Thomas P. Anderson
- Art Puett
- Bobbi Marshall
- Bob Boggs

Dr. Jim Anderson

This book is dedicated to my wife Lori. None of this would have been possible without her love and support.

Thanks for the best 21 years of my life (so far)…!

Table Of Contents

Managing Your Customers Is Part Of A Product Manager's Job

As though being a product manager was not tough enough, it turns out that not only do we have to manage our products, but we also have to manage our customers. Customers don't particularly want to be managed and so they are not necessarily going to make this an easy task for us to accomplish.

In order to manage customers, first we need to have customers. What this means for a product manager that we are going to have to come up with ways to transform prospects into paying customers. Customers come with a lot of customer data. If we want to have any hope of understanding who our customers are or what they want, we're going to have to come up with a way to get all of that customer information into the same database.

All too often product managers like to point out their most loyal customers as one of their most valuable assets. However, it turns out that these customers may not be very profitable. Instead, we need to allow all of our customers to show us how our product can become even better.

Every customer starts out as a prospect. In order to turn them into a customer it is going to take both time and effort. The big question that product managers face is just exactly how much time is it worth to put into a given prospect in order to turn them into a customer? Once you've successfully landed a customer, they will start to use the current version of your product. When you upgrade your product to the next version, it's going to be the product manager's job to find a way to get your customer to also upgrade.

In order for a customer to make the decision to buy your product, they are going to have to carefully evaluate all of the product information that they have. Successful product managers know that in order to speed this process up, they have to be careful to not give their customers too much information.

For more information on what it takes to be a great product manager, check out my blog, The Accidental Product Manager, at:

www.TheAccidentalPM.com

Good luck!

- Dr. Jim Anderson

About The Author

I must confess that I never set out to be a product manager. When I went to school, I studied Computer Science and thought that I'd get a nice job programming and that would be that. Well, at least part of that plan worked out!

My first job was working for Boeing on their F/A-18 fighter jet program. I spent my days programming fighter jet software in assembly language and I loved it. The U.S. government decided to save some money and went looking for other countries to sell this plane to. This put me into an unfamiliar role: I started to meet with foreign military officials in order to explain what my product did.

Time moved on and so did I. I found myself working for Siemens, the big German telecommunications company. They were making phone switches and selling them to the seven U.S. phone companies. The problem was that the switches were too complicated. Customers couldn't tell the difference between one complicated phone switch from another complicated phone switch.

The Siemens sales folks were in a bind. They didn't know enough about how the switches worked to tell their customers why they should buy them. Siemens reached out into their engineering unit looking for anyone who could help the sales teams out. I put my hand up and overnight I became a product manager.

Since then I've spent over 20 years working as a product manager for both big companies and startups. This has given me an opportunity to do everything that a product manager does many, many times. I know what works as well as what doesn't work.

I now live in Tampa Florida where I spend my time managing my consulting business, Blue Elephant Consulting, teaching college courses at the Florida Polytechnic University, and traveling to work with companies like yours to share the knowledge that I have about how product managers can make their product be a success.

I'm always available to answer questions and I can be reached at:

Dr. Jim Anderson
Blue Elephant Consulting
Email: jim@BlueElephantConsulting.com
Facebook: http://goo.gl/1TVoK
Web: **www.BlueElephantConsulting.com**

"Unforgettable communication skills that will set your ideas free…"

Create Products Your Customers Want At A Price That They Are Willing To Pay!

Dr. Jim Anderson is available to provide training and coaching on the two topics that are the most important to product managers everywhere: how do I create the products that my customers want and what should I price them at?

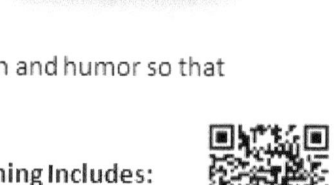

Dr. Anderson believes that in order to both learn and remember what he says, product managers need to laugh. Each one of his speeches is full of fun and humor so that what he says "sticks" with everyone.

Dr. Anderson's Product Management Training Includes:

1. How can you segment your market?
2. What problems are your customers having right now?
3. Which of your customer's problems does your product solve?
4. How much of this problem does your product solve?
5. How much will it cost your customer if they don't fix this problem?

Dr. Jim Anderson presents over 100 speeches per year. To invite Dr. Anderson to speak at your event, contact him at:

Phone: 813-418-6970 or
Email: jim@BlueElephantConsulting.com

Blue Elephant Consulting

Speaking   Negotiating   Managing   Marketing

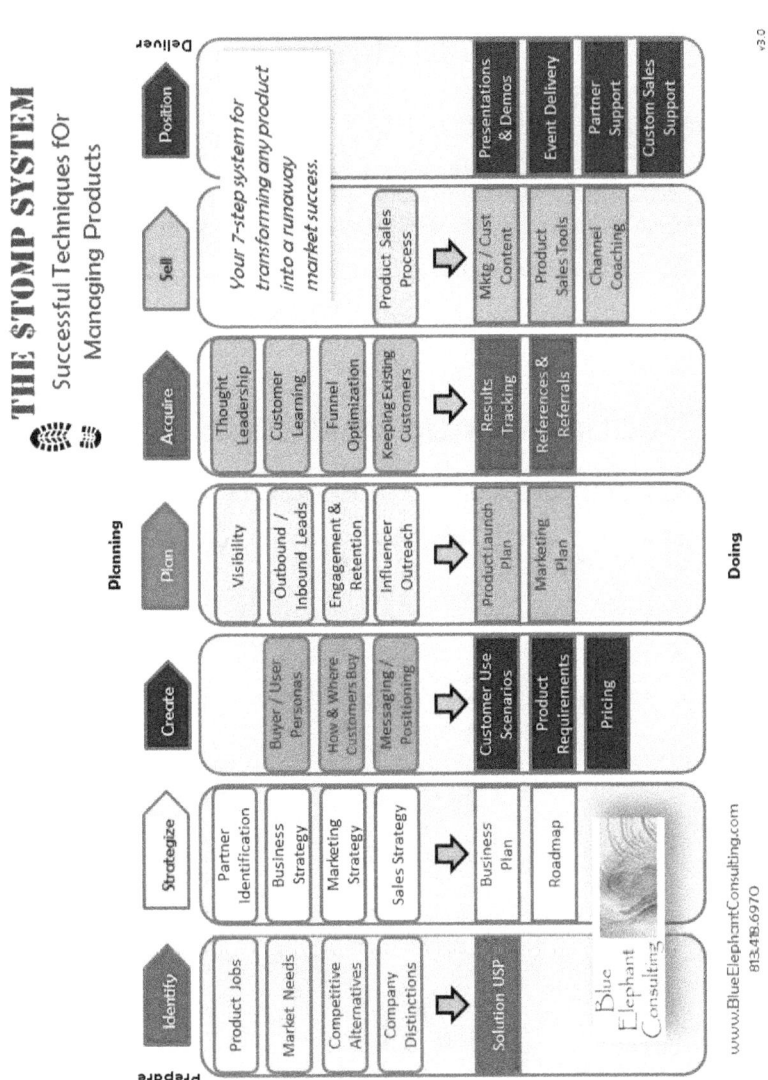

The **$TOMP** product management system has been created by **Blue Elephant Consulting** to help product managers know what to do and when to do it in order for a product to be successful.

Chapter 1

Product Management 101: How The Bar Rescue TV Show Can Teach You How To Turn Prospects Into Clients

Chapter 1: Product Management 101: How The Bar Rescue TV Show Can Teach You How To Turn Prospects Into Clients

We're going to kick it old school this time around and take a look at one of the key skills that every product manager should be good at, but all too often we've been working so hard that we've neglected this task: turning prospects into actual paying customers. If you can't already list this skill on your product manager resume, then when we are done here you'll be able to...

The Wrong Way To Do It: AIDA

After all of my years of being a product manager, I have come to one blindingly obvious conclusion about my customers that shapes everything that I do. My customers don't buy my product. Rather **they buy what my product can do for them**.

This means that every account manager that I end up working with needs to have the same goal that I do: how can I motivate a prospect to get them to **become a customer**? Yeah, yeah – we product managers can talk all day about this feature or that feature of our product, but if we do we are forgetting something that should have been listed on everyone's product manager job description: product management will always be an emotional job because our customers will always buy based on emotions, not logic.

Oh sure, after their gut has told them what product to select they'll come back around and build a fancy logic framework **to support their emotion-based decision**, but it will all be a lie. Armed with this knowledge, what is a product manager to do?

When it comes to the strategic management of prospects, it turns out that our brothers and sisters in the Sales profession have known about this emotionally-guided decision making process for a long time. They've **developed a framework** for guiding prospects and turning them into customers that we should all be following today (you are, aren't you?) in every piece of product-related material that we produce.

Ask any business development manager and they'll tell you that the traditional process of generating customers **starts by getting their attention**. Next you want to generate interest in them (sometimes referred to as creating arousal). This is followed by sparking desire for your product or service. Finally, it all wraps up with a call for action – what steps do you want the prospect to take in order to become a customer? The whole process is referred to as AIDA (awareness, interest, desire, action).

The problem with the AIDA approach is that things are **left pretty wide open for interpretation** as to exactly how to go about doing it. What's the real difference between awareness and desire? You get my point – nice acronym, but tough to put into practice in the real-world.

The Right Way To Do It: Promise & Proof

I've got some good news for you. It turns out that there's **a better way** to go about turning your prospects into customers. Business consultant Herman Holtz identified a two-step process that achieves the same goals.

His process consisted of the following **two steps**: making promise to your customer and then providing the proof that you'll be able to deliver on that promise to them. Perhaps an example would help to make this system clearer.

A current TV show, Bar Rescue, deals with a consultant visiting failing bars and helping them to win more customers and become profitable again. The show's star, Jon Taffer, has a very interesting way of looking at just exactly what product a restaurant is selling. He believes that a restaurant is selling **human reactions**: if you don't react to a plate of food then the restaurant has failed. If you smile, then the restaurant has succeeded.

This is exactly where the **promise / proof technique** comes in to play. The key to this approach is exactly what we've been talking about: people will buy your product not because of what it is, but rather because of what they can do with it. They don't want to own it – they want to enjoy what they can do with it.

So what are you offering to your customers in all of those brochures, web sites, flyers, etc. that you spend your time making? Is it the product and a price? Nope, in reality your offer to your prospect is **the benefit** that you say that your product can deliver. Your prospect wants to know how they can gain the benefit that you are promising them that your product will deliver.

Ultimately it's all going to come down to **the proof that you'll be able to deliver**. Your prospects are going to need to see proof that your product can deliver on the promise that you are making. This means that you need to use certifications, testimonials, reviews, logical arguments, authoritative statements, and guarantees to turn your prospects into customers.

What All Of This Means For You

Taking a quick look around the product management ecosystem, you can find a lot of suggestions for how product managers can get their products noticed by potential customers (a.k.a prospects). What's been missing is how product managers can help to **turn those prospects into paying customers**.

Traditionally product managers have been taught to use the following **four steps** in order to attract prospects and turn them into customers: attention, interest, desire, and action (AIDA). The problem with this approach is that it has always been rather unclear how to actually go about doing it.

I'm proposing that product managers adopt a new approach: **promise and proof**. This is much simpler and immediately gets to the point. This approach requires a product manager to crawl into a customer's mind and really understand what promise they view the product as delivering. Once this is understood, the next step is to provide the almost-customer with the proof that they need in order to commit to selecting your product.

Now that you have this understanding of the role that a product manager has in turning prospects into customers, you need to **go out there and do it**. No, you are not in sales, but you are part of the team that is responsible for making sure that your product is a success. Good luck!

Chapter 2

Product Managers Are Learning The Marketing Power Of One (Database)

Chapter 2: Product Managers Are Learning The Marketing Power Of One (Database)

All too often Product Managers fool themselves into thinking that **more is better**. Yes, sometimes this may be true, but when it comes to keeping track of both customers and product inventory, it turns out that using one database is the key to long term success...

How Things Can Get Out Of Hand

Although we often talk about this problem when it comes to launching new products, it turns out that it can also affect **older products** – it just sneaks up on them. In both cases, things start out ok and then take a turn for the worse.

When a company starts to sell a product, they always seem to start with **an initial sales channel.** Your product's account manager and business development manager will be working hard to make this channel a success. In this modern age in which we are living, it can very well be an e-commerce channel right off the bat. Customers who purchase the product using this channel will provide the company with a great deal of information about themselves. This information will then be stored in the e-commerce channel's systems and databases. This all seems like a standard part of any product manager's product manager job description, right?

If the company chooses to **expand this channel**, for example adding a gift card program, this additional functionality may come with its own database for retaining information about the customers that interact with it. Now things are starting to get out of hand. Throw in some strategic management and you'll quickly find yourself adding in-store purchase data collection and tracking systems and perhaps an inventory management system and you'll discover that things have completely gotten out of hand.

Once product and customer information has been spread out among so many different systems, **problems can start to show up** such as products being out-of-stock but the ordering systems not showing that when customers place an order. Many companies try to overcome the limitations of this type of solution by having people manually type information that is in one system into the other systems; however, even under the best of situations there is a time lag here. That means that your product's inventory levels can change and your potential customers won't know about it until after they have placed their orders.

The Power Of One (Database)

So what's a product manager to do? Good question. It turns out that the solution is easy to recognize, hard to implement. What a product manager needs to do is to move to using **one single database** to handle all of the information related to their product.

What you should be looking for is a single database that can hold all of the **cross-channel sales data** along with any inventory data that your company has on your product. By implementing a solution like this, product managers will be able to offer their customers a real-time order management solution along with an improved customer experience.

Once a single database view of your product has been put into place, you'll be able to do things as a product manager that you were never able to do before. The first thing is that you'll be able to engage in true **cross-channel marketing** and selling of your product: you'll know what's going on so you'll be able to tell the correct story to the correct channel.

Next, you'll be prepared to move into the m-commerce (mobile) space. Making it easier for your customers to both buy your product and check on the status of their orders. Finally, **the customer's buying experience will be improved** because company staff will have access to all of the information about both a customer's order and your product's inventory that will be needed to answer any questions that come up.

What All Of This Means For You

Product managers know that for a product to be successful, they are going to have to **develop multiple channels** to sell it. Once this process starts, it can be all too easy to start to create multiple databases that don't talk to each other.

The problem with this is that once you start to spread important customer and product data across multiple databases, it become almost impossible to get an accurate picture of how your product is doing. Product managers need to take the time and make the effort to **consolidate all of these databases into a single database**.

This single database will allow them to overcome the cross-channel inventory disparity that can hold back their cross-channel sales efforts. Making the effort will result in **the creation of an even more successful product. Now that's something that you can add to your product manager resume!**

Chapter 3

Product Managers Need To Understand That Loyal Customers Are Not Always Profitable Customers

Chapter 3: Product Managers Need To Understand That Loyal Customers Are Not Always Profitable Customers

Every product manager out there **would like to have more customers**. In fact, the best kind of customer that we'd like to have are those rare and elusive loyal customers. When we are working on our product development definition, we all figure that the more of those that we're able to pick up, the more profitable our product will be. Good guess, but you'd be wrong...

Why Loyalty Doesn't Equal Profitability

What does it mean to be a "loyal" customer? I think that we can all agree that it means that a customer feels some sort of bond towards either your company or to your product. We all believe that the more of these that we can get, the better its going to look on our product manager resume. However, studies have shown that **this is not enough** for a customer to be a profitable customer.

Timothy Keiningham and others have been researching what makes a customer both loyal and profitable. What they have discovered is that a large number of customers that product managers believe are loyal **are not even profitable customers**. It turns out that how your customers feel about your product is a poor predictor of how they'll behave towards your product (like buy it).

Here's the harsh part. Studies have shown that over half of your so-called loyal customers' loyalty is driven by expectations that they can **get a great deal from you**. These customers turn out to not be profitable customers for you to have.

If you ran the world, then all of your customers **would be both loyal and profitable**. However, you don't and it turns out that a lot of your customers are not fitting this description. In fact the researchers have discovered that the customers that you want, the profitable ones, generally only make up about 20% of your customer base, break-even customers make up 60% of your customer base, and unprofitable customers make up the remaining 20%.

How Product Managers Can Get More Profitable Loyals

So there you are – you've got a whole bunch of customers that prior to reading this article you thought were both loyal and profitable. Now you know that just because they are loyal customers doesn't mean that they are profitable customers. **What's a product manager to do?**

It's pretty simple really. What you are going to want to do is to **increase the number of profitable loyals** – those customers who are both loyal and who are profitable for you. That means that you're going to want to have more customers who feel positively about your product while at the same time have a positive value to the company (they spend more on your product than you spend on servicing them).

In order to transform some of your loyal customers into profitable loyal customers, **you are going to have to take action**. You're going to have to do some research in order to determine what is holding back customers who think highly of your product from spending more money on your product.

Don't forget that conducting a survey of your existing customers can yield additional results. You may be able to determine what is holding your profitable loyal customers back from **spending even more money on your products**. If you are able to find ways to make your product appeal more to both sets of customers, then your product's bottom line should benefit.

What All Of This Means For You

We all know that **getting new customers for our products** is both time consuming and expensive. However, we used to think that if we could identify a customer as being a loyal customer then we had it made – our product would have to be profitable. In fact, getting more loyal customers is often a part of a product manager job description.

Research has shown that this is not the case – many customers who we would identify as being "loyal" customers **turn out to not be profitable for us**. What this means for product managers is that we need to take steps to work with our loyal customers in order to turn them into profitable loyal customers.

The first step in making your product more profitable is **understanding who your best customers are**. Loyal customers can play a big role in the success of your product. However, first you need to make sure that your loyal customers are really your profitable customers!

Chapter 4

---

4 Ways Product Managers Can Let Their Customers Make Their Product A Success

Chapter 4: 4 Ways Product Managers Can Let Their Customers Make Their Product A Success

The one thing that every product manager wants more than anything else in this world is **for our product to be a success —** this should almost be a part of the product development definition. We are willing to work very hard to make this happen. However, maybe we've got it all wrong – it's not what we do that will make our product a success, but rather what our customers do. Let's take a look and see how we can let them show us what we need to be doing...

Welcome To The World Of Social Web Sites

One of the biggest advantages of living in the 21st Century is that we've got **this great thing called the Internet**. All of a sudden, product managers now have an easy way to both get and stay in contact with the customers of their product. Having a communications channel like this is great; however, it doesn't come with any operating instructions...

All too often, product managers **try to control how our customers use the Internet to talk about our product**. What a lot of us have done is to set up web sites where our customers can come and talk about our product. However, that's it – all we want them to do is talk about our product. Oh, and don't you even think about saying something bad about the product – we're going to tightly police what is said and delete any negative comments.

The end result of these kinds of actions are **rarely visited web sites** that are of no value to your customers or to you. This is not something that you're going to want to put on your product manager resume. It turns out that there are other types of social web sites out there that discuss products (such as those that talk about just about any Apple product) that are wildly popular. What's the difference between these two types of web sites?

4 Ways To Create A Brand Community For Your Product

The big difference is that those other web sites have been successful in building a so-called **"brand community"**. This is a site where customers can learn more about a product, discuss problems and how to solve them, and talk with other people who use the product.

I'm going to guess that you'd like to be able to create a successful online brand community for your product. If so, then you're going to need to follow the following **four steps** to create a successful social web site for your product:

Hand's Off!: When you set up a social web site for your product, you get to set the rules. However, if you limit the discussion to only product-related items or if you prohibit negative comments about your product, you'll be shooting yourself in your foot. A social web site is just that – social. Let your customers talk about what they want to talk about – they'll always eventually come back to talking about your product. Also, let them make negative comments about the product. Both of these types of discussions will provide you with great insights into both your customers and how they are using your product.

Keep It Diverse: Who do you really want to come and visit your product's social web site? Do you really think that your market segmentation is 100% correct? Don't limit use of your web site to one particular type of customer or even to people who have already bought your product. Instead, throw the doors open and let anyone who has an interest in your product participate. This is when the real learning for you will occur.

It's Not A Support Site: If your social web site was just an extension of your customer support department, then visitors could open trouble tickets and get them answered. Instead, you need to provide your customers with ways to interact and communicate with other visitors. Don't make it a customer-to-company discussion, make it a anyone-to-anyone discussion – that's what "social" is all about.

Unofficial Is Ok Too: There is no way that there will only be one web site that deals with your product. In fact, there may be many others. As a product manager you're going to need to come up with a plan to at least monitor what is being said about your product on these other sites. An even better plan is to participate in them. Become a contributor and you'll be able to harness their customer feedback in addition to your own site.

What All Of This Means For You

As a product manager, we can accomplish a lot. However, we may not be able to make our product a success simply by our own actions. Instead, it turns out that **we need the help of our customers**.

We can get the feedback that we need from our customers by **creating social web sites** that they can use to talk about, among other things, our products. However, in order for these types of sites to be effective, we need to follow the four things that we've discussed. The ability to set up this kind of effective customer communications channel will probably soon become a part of every product manager job description.

We live in fantastic times – never before have product managers had so many tools that can allow us to connect with our customers. However, we need to **learn how to use these tools correctly** so that we can ensure that our products will be the success that we know that they can be.

Chapter 5

Product Managers Need To Know How Much Time To Invest In A Prospect

Chapter 5: Product Managers Need To Know How Much Time To Invest In A Prospect

Talk to any product manager and they can tell you, when a new product gets introduced, the product manager **becomes a part of the sales team** for at least awhile – that's almost a part of the product development definition. What this really means is that you are going to get caught up in the process of talking to and helping to prepare estimate / RFP responses for prospective customers. Is this really the best way for you to be spending your time?

Cost vs Benefit

The reason that we're having this talk today is because one of my readers reached out to me with a common product manager complaint. His point was that he believed that he was **spending way too much time** working with prospective clients because only a small number of them ever actually turned into paying clients in the end. This wasn't something that he was going to be able to add to his product manager resume.

We got to talking and he admitted that he was grateful that his product was generating enough interest that he had this problem. However, he was wondering if he (or his sales team) was doing something wrong because they weren't able to **convert more of these prospects into customers**.

We got to talking and my first question to him was "what is your conversion rate" – how many of these prospects are you turning into customers? He reported that he was only able to turn about 21% of these prospects into customers. Well now – it turns out that his product must be a fantastic product because every product manager's goal should be to **turn one out of every 5 prospects into a paying customer** – and he was doing better than this!

My reader indicated that he **was spending his time in a number of different ways**. He'd talk with customers when they first expressed an interest in his product (sales would hand them off to him because the product was so new). He'd create an estimate for them as the next step. If the prospect liked the estimate, then he'd create a full blown proposal for them. He would also follow up with the prospects who received an estimate but who didn't request a proposal.

How To Get The Best Return On Your Time

I spent some time with my reader going over **how much time each step in his process was taking him**. We figured out how much his company was paying him per hour and did some rough back-of-the-envelope calculations.

What we were trying to do here was to figure out **just how expensive it was** for him to be spending his time working on those estimates and proposals that were not resulting in a paying customer. In the end it turned out that these lost prospects came out to be roughly 7% of the sales of his product.

Now 7% of the sales of your product may or may not seem like a lot of money to you. I would ask that he not view this as lost money. Instead, it's better to view it as being a type of investment – perhaps **a specialized type of advertising** that is helping him to acquire the 1 out of 5 customers that he is getting.

However, there was **one key learning lesson** to be had from all of this analysis. He was spending too much time trying to reach out to the prospects that got estimates but who did not request a full proposal. His efforts to contact them were not really having any positive results and he already had enough customers. This was clearly not the best use of his time. If his company thought that it was important to do this, then have the sales teams make those calls.

What All Of This Means For You

Product managers will often get drawn into the sales process when a new product is introduced. Although this may not be a part of your product manager job description, it turns out that this is only natural because we are the ones who know the most about the product. However, this can **take up a great deal of your valuable time**.

What product managers need to do when they are feeling overwhelmed is to **run some numbers**. Take a look at how many of the prospects that you are dealing with are turning into actual customers. If you are anywhere near the 20% mark, then consider yourself lucky – you are right where you need to be.

If you are spending your time trying to **chase the prospects that "got away"**, you may want to rethink your actions. Depending on how close you are to the 20% conversion point, it may not be worth your time to be chasing these potential customers. Take a look around your company and see if there is any other department that might be better suited to taking on this task.

Chapter 6

Product Managers Need To Understand How To Upgrade Customers

Chapter 6: Product Managers Need To Understand How To Upgrade Customers

One of the joys of being a product manager is that our products are always getting better. What this means for our customers is **a never ending cycle of upgrades**. Something that is probably not talked about enough is the issue of how to get your customers to upgrade (although we do this so often that it really should be part of the product development definition). You really don't want to have to support old versions of your product for very long, but customers fear change. What's product manager to do?

The Problems With Upgrades

When we make our product better, it only stands to reason that our existing customers **should be excited** to get their hands on the new and better version of our product, right? Getting them to accept our latest upgrade should be something that each of us should be able to put on our product manager resume. Every time that we upgrade our product, the new version is going to be better in some way: faster, simpler, etc. However, there's a problem here.

The problem with upgrades, from our customer's point of view, is that **the upgrade is different**. If we've made a lot of changes to our product, then it's possible that it may feel like an entirely new product. The upgrade represents change – and nobody likes change.

As product managers, when we show up on our existing customer's doorstep and start to tell them how great our new and improved product is, we need to be careful. From our customer's vantage point, having a new product does not necessarily translate into **having a better product**. Rather, what it means is that we have a different product. Customers don't always see different as being a good thing.

How A Product Manager Should Handle An Upgrade

Upgrades happen. Upgrades are a part of life. As product managers it is in our own best interest to find ways for our customers to go ahead and **accept our latest upgrade** – among other things it can help to lower our costs of supporting multiple versions of our product.

How best to go about doing this is where things get tricky. Jason Fried is a co-founder of the online software company 37Signals and they recently went through a radical software upgrade process and **learned a great deal in the process**.

The most fundamental thing that they learned was that when it comes to upgrades, **time is critical**. New ideas like your product upgrade will take time for your customers to get used to. The last thing in the world that you want to do is to try to talk your customers into upgrading the version of your product that they are using when they are in the middle of using your product for some big project that they are involved in.

Instead, Jason reports, a better way to get your customers to accept your new product upgrade is to **give them time**. One way to do this is to invite them to check out the new version of your product without requiring them to upgrade to it. Let them discover what features it has that they'll want to have. Given enough time, your customers can talk themselves into doing the upgrade – you won't have to push them to do it.

What All Of This Means For You

Products change – we improve them and they get better. This means that our customers who are using older versions of our products **need to upgrade our product every so often**. This can pose a challenge for them. Most product managers don't know how to deal with this situation – it was never part of our product manager job description.

Nobody like change and an upgrade represents a change for our customers. The wrong way to go about managing a product upgrade is to **force or push our customers to make the change**. They'll just end up pushing back. Instead, we need to take the time and let them check out the upgraded product. Let them discover why it's better and why they should upgrade. Then let them make the switch when they are ready to do so.

Allowing our customers to control when they upgrade the version of our product that they are using is **the key to a successful upgrade**. As long as they feel that they are in control, the upgrade will go smoothly and they won't complain the next time that you show up with an upgrade – because you know that you will!

Chapter 7

Product Managers Know Customers Don't Buy When You Tell Them Too Much

Chapter 7: Product Managers Know Customers Don't Buy When You Tell Them Too Much

If you would like to get more of your potential customers to buy your product, what's **the best way to make this happen**? If you talked with product managers, I'd be willing to bet that you'd hear a lot of them tell you that delivering more product information to your potential customers just might do the trick. I've heard this so often I've almost come to believe that it's a part of the product development definition. It turns out that this is dead wrong...

What The Experiments Show

This kind of discussion can quickly go down a rat hole with me saying one thing and you thinking something completely different. That's why I think that we need to go **have a talk with the scientists**.

What the scientists have discovered is that when your customers get presented with too much information, they do the one thing that you don't want them to do. **They shut down**. They decide to skip making a purchase altogether because it's "...just too difficult to make a decision..." That's not the kind of thing that you're going to want to have to put on your product manager resume.

In a now classic experiment, some scientists went to a grocery store and gave shoppers a choice between 6 types of a product. 30% of the customers went on to make a purchase. When the scientists **boosted the number of types of products that they showed to shoppers to 24**, then only 3% of the shoppers went on to make a purchase.

What psychologists have discovered is that when you give your potential customers too much information, **bad things happen**. Customers feel indecision, angst, regret and will eventually end up with a lower sense of satisfaction with both the process of purchasing your product and your product itself.

What Overthinking Can Do To Sales Of Your Product

It turns out that your potential customers are already complaining about **being hit with way too much information** about everybody's products and services.

Although you may be looking for ways **to better "engage" with your customers**, there is a very good chance that this is the one thing that they don't want you to do! If you overload your potential customers with too much product information, it may end up backfiring on you.

There is another ugly truth to this too much information issue. It turns out that the more information about our product that we provide to our customers, **the harder it is going to be for them to be able to make a decision about it**.

When it becomes hard to make a decision, then the more information that you provide them with, **the more important your customer is going to believe that the decision is**. This will end up causing them to spend more time and effort trying to make a decision. This will lead them to believing that it's an even more important decision.

All of this is going to cause your customers to become **more and more upset** about the decision that they are going to be making. Long after the decision is made, your customers are still going to be looking for ways to validate the decision that they made.

What All Of This Means For You

Every product manager would like for their product to be more popular – they'd like more potential customers to turn into real customers. A simple way of making this happen would seem to just **create and deliver more product information** so that people would choose your product. Seems like this should be a part of every product manager job description.

However, research has shown that **this will have the opposite effect**. Too much information causes potential customers to have a harder time making a decision. They start to overthink even the smallest of decisions and in the end they'll regret any decision that they do make.

Product managers need to carefully look at how their potential customers are going about **making their buying decisions**. They need to simplify the process as much as possible and only provide the information that is truly needed. Listen to your customer and provide them with just enough information to simplify their decision making process.

Chapter 8

Product Managers Need To Learn To K.I.S.S. Their Customers

Chapter 8: Product Managers Need To Learn To K.I.S.S. Their Customers

Doggone it – what do your customers really want? You try listening to them, you try sending them surveys, you meet them at trade shows, and yet you still feel as though **they just don't quite understand how great your product really is** and so they aren't buying it. You've done everything that is included in the product development definition, what's a product manager to do?

K.I.S.S.

I sure hope that you've heard of **the K.I.S.S principle** by now. What? You haven't? Well, then perhaps some education is called for. The acronym K.I.S.S. stands for the phrase "Keep It Simple Stupid".

Knowing what this really means should be something that is on every product manager resume.

What this means for product managers is that we need to search for ways to **make it easy for our customers to buy our products**. In this day and age of ever increasing marketing messages that we create and throw at our customers, this may not be so easy to do.

Remember, what needs to happen for a customer to actually buy your product is part of **a complicated set of steps**. They need to become aware of your product, decide that it's the right one for them, and then buy it. If we provide our potential customers with too many marketing messages, then they'll become flustered and they'll never get around to that last step – actually making a purchase.

The researchers who study the whole buying process of customers have a name for what it takes to get a customer to **follow through** on an intended purchase – they call it "stickiness". Is your product sticky?

How Do Customers Determine If Your Product Is Simple To Buy?

Make a good product and make it easy to buy and that's exactly what customers will do. However, it's that last part – **make it easy to buy** – that seems to trip a lot of product managers up.

As a product manager, you'd like to be able to **attract and retain sticky customers**. These are the ones who will buy many things from you. Now the big question is how to go about doing this?

The researchers who study sticky customer behavior have come up with a measure of how sticky a customer is and they call it the **"decision simplicity index"**. This index is based on three characteristics of your product's marketing program.

The first is just how easy is it for your customers to **gather information about your product**. They'll be using this information to understand what your product is and what it can do for them.

The next characteristic is just how much they can **trust the information that they have gathered**. This has a lot to do with where the information came from and the type of relationship that the customer has developed with that source over time.

Finally, it all comes down to how easily your customers can **weigh the information that they have gathered**. Not all information is equal and so each piece has to be compared against every other piece and then its relative value has to be determined.

Your job as a product manager is to make this purchase decision journey for your potential customers **easier to do for your product**. The better that you do this, the higher the decision simplicity index will be for your product and the more of your product you will sell.

What Does All Of This Mean For You?

If only being a successful product manager just meant creating the best product, then everything would be simple, right? It turns out that the job is a bit more complex than that – we need to be very careful in **how we communicate with our customers** so that we don't overload them. Even though this is not on any product manager job description, you need to consider it to be part of your job.

Researchers have determined that in order to make a sale to a potential customer, our products need to have **a high decision simplicity index**. This index is based on how easy it is to collect information on our product, how much that information is trusted, and how easy it is to weight the information.

The good news is that controlling how we communicate with our customers is something that **every product manager can do**. However, we need to be very careful that we don't do too much because that will cause our customers to take no action. Pick your words wisely and you'll boost your product's sales!

Chapter 9

Product Managers Need To Make The Product Purchase Process Perfect

Chapter 9: Product Managers Need To Make The Product Purchase Process Perfect

As product managers, we have a responsibility to our potential customers to make the product identification, selection, and purchasing process as easy as possible. However, all too often we seem to get caught up in trying to use **the latest wiz-bang marketing tools** that we've just read about and we can lose sight of just exactly how our customers go about the process of purchasing our product...

Where Is Your Customer At?

Back in product management school (we all went to that didn't we?), right after we learned what the product development definition was we were taught that the buying process is not an instantaneous decision but rather **it is a process** that each customer goes through. In order to understand why potential customers are (or are not) buying your product, you need to have a good understanding of just exactly where they are in this buying process at all times.

In our desire to win over more customers it can be very easy for product managers to make the purchasing path **too confusing** for our customers. If we want to make the purchasing path more efficient, then what we don't have to do is to create the fanciest web site. Rather what we need to find is a way to minimize the number of different information sources that our potential customers will have to come into contact with as they move through the purchasing process for our product.

What you need to do is to collect information. Lots of information. What you are going to be looking for is data from **four modern marketing sources**: ad-effectiveness, monitoring of social media channels, web site clickstream analysis, and campaign-tracking information. Your goal, once you have all of this information, will be to get a feel for the common purchase paths that your customers take when they are looking for a solution to their problem. Get this right and you'll have something to add to your product manager resume.

Once you understand how your customers are going about trying to solve their problem, you can determine **how many of your customers are taking what path**. You can also determine which of the paths instill the greatest amount of confidence in your customers.

Your goal here will be to determine at which point in the process you can provide your customers with what type of product information in order to move them closer to making a buying decision. You'll also be able to determine where in the process your potential customers **may be losing confidence in your product** and may end up giving up or selecting another firm's product.

If you are looking for a magic bullet here, I've got some bad news for you – one does not exist. However, the product managers who do a good job of making it easy for their customers to select and purchase their product do it **by making the purchasing process more personal**.

What Information Does Your Customer Want?

Knowing what information your customers don't want is important; however, its not really all that valuable. What you really need to know is **what information your customers would like to have**.

The key thing to understand when trying to answer this question is that **there really are multiple answers**. Depending on what stage in the purchasing process your customers is at, they'll have a need for a different type of information.

You can expect a customer who is at the start of their search to have a need for more basic, high-level information. This can be determined, for example, by **the type of web searches that they are doing**. An example of this would be a search for "4G LTE mobile phones". Later searches may show that the customer is getting ready to make a decision about their purchase. An example of this kind of search would be "Apple 4 vs Samsung Galaxy S III".

The customers who are looking for general information can be directed by the product manager to product overview documents. However, when the customer is getting close to making a decision, you are going to want to **personalize the process**. You can do this by directing them to a web site where they could get social proof that selecting your product would be the right decision.

What Does All Of This Mean For You?

Our customers do not just wake up one day and decide that they are going to purchase our product. Instead, they go through a process in which they collect information, talk to other people who have solved the same problem, and finally **make a buying decision**.

As product managers, we need to be careful to not **make the purchase process too complex for our customers**. Instead, we want to make sure that they are only presented with the information that they need, when they need it. This means that we need to collect information to understand the purchase process and then we need to provide the right information at the right time. This should really be a part of every product manager job description.

Understanding how our customers come to the conclusion to purchase our products is **the key to long term product success**. We need to take the time to study the purchase process for our product and then make sure that we're spending our product management time in the best way possible in order to ensure that we'll have the greatest success.

Chapter 10

How Product Managers Can Help Their Customers Weigh Their Options

Chapter 10: How Product Managers Can Help Their Customers Weigh Their Options

Have you ever had to make a decision between two products that you were considering buying? How did you go about doing this? If you are like most of us, you collected what data you could on both products and then **you weighed the data** in order to try to see which product would best meet your needs. Just exactly how do your customers go about weighing your product against other products?

More Product Data Does Not Make Product Selection Easier

Just exactly how do your customers go about determining if they want to buy your product? Studies have shown that for products that cost US$50 or more, 25% of customers say that they spend most of their effort on product research. Of this 25%, 20% say that most of their effort is spent **doing comparison shopping**. How are you helping your customers to do this?

As product managers, all too often we think that we are helping our customers make a decision about our product when we really are not. What we tend to do is to **create buying guides for our customers** that list product features so that our customers can choose between our small, medium, and large products.

It turns out that this really does nothing to help our customers. More information is not what our customers are looking for. Rather what they want product managers to do is to help them to **feel confident about the choice that they are trying to make**. What this means is that we need to provide our customers with a way to both identify and then weigh the product features that are the most important to them.

How To Help Your Customer Weigh Your Product

When it comes to helping your customer feel confident that they are making the right decision, one company that has got it right is the diamond company, De Beers. They are the ones who came up with the "4Cs" system of evaluating and comparing diamonds (cut, color, clarity, and caret). This approach took a process that most people know nothing about and provided them with confidence that they were **weighing the essential features** needed to make the right decision.

As product managers we need to help our customers **control the number of features** that enter into their weighting process. Sometimes there may be many, many different features associated with our products and as product managers we need to create ways that will help our customers sort through all of these features in order to identify the ones that really matter to them.

One way to go about doing this is by **adding logic to your product's web site**. You can have the customer provide some basic information about themselves and then use that information to narrow the product configurations that they should be considering. By doing this you will have made it easier for them to weigh their options when making the buying decision.

What All Of This Means For You

Making decisions is hard work and your customers have to make decisions when they are considering whether or not to buy your product. As a product manager, you need to help them with **the product weighing process.**

One thing that too many product managers don't realize is that simply by providing your customers with even more information about your product you won't make the decision making process any easier for them. Instead what you need to do is to provide them with tools that will allow them to **filter the available information** down to just the elements that matter to them.

The easier that you make it for your customers to weigh what your product has to offer against what other products offer, the easier it will be for them to **reach a buying decision**. If they see how simple it is to interact with your product, then it will be cast in a favorable light. When that happens, you'll have more customers selecting your product and that is what it takes to make a product manager happy!

Chapter 11

What Can A Tax Software Company Teach Product Managers About Customer Information Overload?

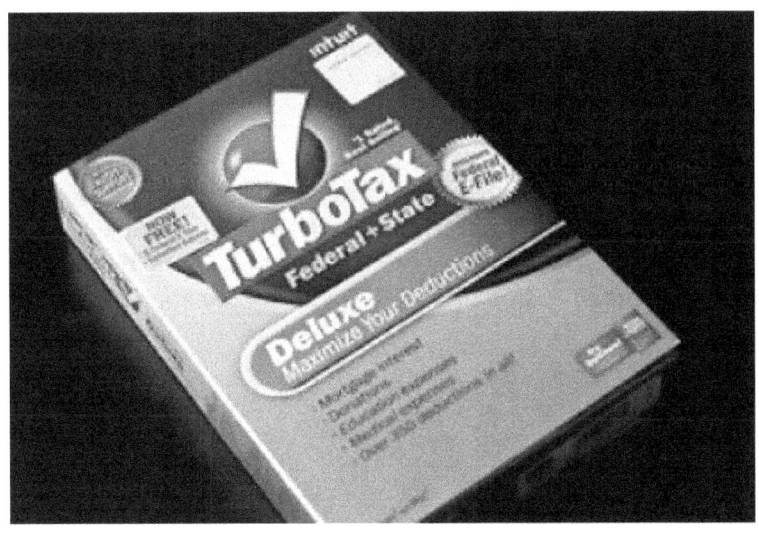

Chapter 11: What Can A Tax Software Company Teach Product Managers About Customer Information Overload?

Ugg, taxes! I don't like them, you don't like them, nobody likes them. One of the reasons that nobody likes taxes is that they are so **very complicated** – what counts as taxable income and what doesn't? It turns out that the company Intuit realized that we don't like taxes and they've made a lot of money with their TurboTax software that many of us in the USA use to prepare our taxes. There's a lesson for us product managers to learn from the world of tax preparation software – make it easy to select your product and you'll be very successful.

Finding Your Way

The more difficult the problem that your product addresses, the more complex it is going to be for your potential customers to determine if they want to buy it. This is almost a part of the standard product development definition. That's why you need to create product information navigation tools that they can use to **make their decision making process simpler**.

Over at Intuit they accomplished this for their TurboTax product by creating the **"TurboTax Live Community"** where people who have either bought the software or who are considering buying it can come to get answers to their questions. This allows Intuit to provide their customers with the right information at exactly the right time.

Building Trust

Nobody is going to buy your product until they trust that it will solve their problems and they trust that you'll stand behind your product if they have any problems with it. In order to have any chance of being successful and boosting your product manager resume you are going to have to get your customers to believe what you are telling them. This means that your potential customers **really need to hear from other customers**.

Intuit helps this to happen by hosting over 160,000 user generated reviews of their TurboTax product on its website. **Not all of these reviews are positive** – there are number of one star reviews. However, because these low rating reviews exist, a customer visiting the site will believe the other reviews. The more that potential customers see that people just like them are buying and using the product, the more likely they are to make a purchase.

Making A Decision

When all of the available information has been collected, it is time for your potential customers to weigh it and then **make a decision**. This can be the toughest part of the buying process. The more products, configurations, and options that you have, the more difficult it is for your customers to make a decision to buy.

Intuit attempts to solve this problem by **providing a comparison chart** of their products presented in a side-by-side fashion. This simplifies the process of making a comparison. They also allow customers to select boxes that indicate what features are important to them and it then helps them to make a decision about what product to buy.

What All Of This Means For You

Complex products create **complex decisions** for our customers. As product managers it is part of our product manager job description to take steps to simplify the process of evaluating and selecting our product as much as possible.

Intuit, the company that makes the TurboTax software, has done this very well. They've helped their customers to **navigate through all of the available product information**. They've taken steps to allow other customer's review of their product to act as social proof for potential customers. Finally, they've helped their customers to make a decision by presenting their products in a way that makes side-by-side comparisons easy to do.

Complex products solve complex problems and so our customers truly do need our products. However, they are not going to buy them if they can't figure out if our product is going to solve their problem. Take the time to understand how your customer is going to go about **making their buying decision** and then take steps to simplify this process for them.

Chapter 12

Product Managers Need To Learn How To Offer Customers A Next Best Offer

Chapter 12: Product Managers Need To Learn How To Offer Customers A Next Best Offer

If there was a perfect world for us product managers to live in, what would it look like? Sure there would be white unicorns everywhere but what would our jobs be like? I'd guess that **we'd know our customers much better than we know them today**. In a perfect world, starting with the product development definition, product managers would be able to target their customers with the perfectly customized offer at exactly the right time across the right set of channels. Does this perfect world exist?

Just Exactly What Is A "Next Best Offer"?

Product managers have always wanted to be able to **read their customer's mind**. Here in the 21st Century it's starting to look like we just might be able to do this. The arrival of analytics is providing product managers with mountains of data about their customer's preferences and how they go about the process of shopping. However studies show that most of us are not making good use of all of this data.

Back in the old days, if they indeed ever existed, your customers would form a healthy relationship with your product's sales team. They would have discussions about what the customer was trying to accomplish with their business and your skilled and knowledgeable sales team could **guide the customer to the product or configuration that would best meet their needs**.

Sadly, this situation rarely exists these days. Instead, your customers have **too little time** to develop these types of relationships and you have too many and too complex products for your sales teams to have a good understanding of all of them.

What all of this means is that all too often, your customers are going to **find themselves on their own** when they are trying to find a way to solve the problem that they are facing. This is where product managers need to step in and start to offer Next Best Offers (NBO). Do this right and you'll have something that you can add to your product manager resume.

A Next Best Offer is based on all of that demographic and psychographic information that you are probably already collecting on your customers. You use this to **create a highly customized offer** that will steer your customers to the right configuration of your product. This is what we call a Next Best Offer.

In the brave new world that product managers are living in, we may be tempted to go after a bunch of goals using all of the new consumer analytics data that we now have. However, **a Next Best Offer program** offers us the best value in terms of both potential ROI and enhanced competitiveness.

How Can Product Managers Define Our Objectives?

If we are going to get the most out of our NBO efforts, we're going to have to start in the right place. The experts agree that before we do anything else, we first have to **create clear objectives** for our NBO program.

If you want to have any hope of coming up with clear objectives for an NBO program, then you are going to have to be able to answer the simple question **"What do you want to achieve?"** The good news is that there is no one right answer to this question.

Depending on what your company's current goals are, **you may have to choose between many different answers to this question**. You may be trying to increase the revenues that your product brings in. You may trying to boost the loyalty of the customers that you already have. You may want to get more money from the customers that you already have. Perhaps you simply want more new customers.

No matter which objective best meets your needs, **you need to choose one** that you can use when you are trying to figure out how to use your customer data in order to make the perfect offer to your customers. However, there is one more thing that you need to understand.

As with all things in marketing, the objective that you select that you'll be using to achieve product success with is not set in concrete. This means that there is a good chance that **your market conditions will change on you at some point in time**. When this happens, you need to make sure that you've remained flexible enough to modify what your objective is.

What Does All Of This Mean For You?

In a perfect world, a part of every product manager job description would state we were to instinctively know what kind of solution our customers were searching for in order to solve their problems. We don't live in a perfect world so we need to collect as much data about our customers as we can and then **use analytics** to determine how we can best serve them.

However, all too often we don't do a good job of accomplishing this. What we would like to be able to do is to present our customers with the correct Next Best Offer which we defined as being the right offer at the right time across the right channels. However, this won't be possible for us to do if we haven't **taken the time to choose the correct objectives**.

Having a great deal of customer data is a great feeling. However, all of that data is not going to do us any good unless we are able to find a way to transform it into **actionable customer knowledge**. Creating Next Best Offers is the best way to go about doing this.

It's from the forge of failure that the steel of success is formed.

Hard Work Does Not Guarantee Success, But Success Does Not Happen Without Hard Work.

- Dr. Jim Anderson

Create Products Your Customers Want At A Price That They Are Willing To Pay!

Dr. Jim Anderson is available to provide training and coaching on the two topics that are the most important to product managers everywhere: how do I create the products that my customers want and what should I price them at?

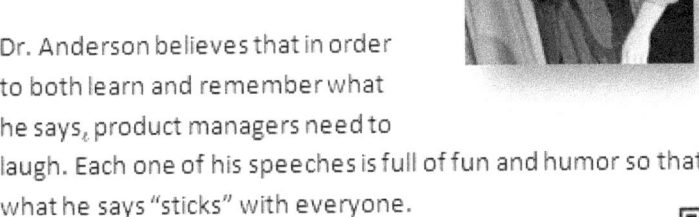

Dr. Anderson believes that in order to both learn and remember what he says, product managers need to laugh. Each one of his speeches is full of fun and humor so that what he says "sticks" with everyone.

Dr. Anderson's Product Management Training Includes:

1. How can you segment your market?
2. What problems are your customers having right now?
3. Which of your customer's problems does your product solve?
4. How much of this problem does your product solve?
5. How much will it cost your customer if they don't fix this problem?

Dr. Jim Anderson presents over 100 speeches per year. To invite Dr. Anderson to speak at your event, contact him at:

Phone: 813-418-6970 or
Email: jim@BlueElephantConsulting.com

Blue Elephant Consulting
Speaking   Negotiating   Managing   Marketing

Photo Credits:

Cover - Colony of Gamers

https://www.flickr.com/photos/colonyofgamers/

Chapter 1 - John Colby

https://www.flickr.com/photos/johncolby/

Chapter 2 - Justin McGregor

https://www.flickr.com/photos/skippytpe/

Chapter 3 – stavos

https://www.flickr.com/photos/stavos52093/

Chapter 4 - ceneal1

https://morguefile.com/p/684118

Chapter 5 - William Warby

https://www.flickr.com/photos/wwarby/

Chapter 6 – Bobcatnorth

https://www.flickr.com/photos/bobcatnorth/

Chapter 7 - doctor_bob

https://morguefile.com/p/55386

Chapter 8 - Laurie Pink

https://www.flickr.com/photos/laurie_pink/

Chapter 9 - antony_mayfield

https://www.flickr.com/photos/antonymayfield/

Chapter 10 - Sepehr Ehsani

https://www.flickr.com/photos/sepehrehsani/

Chapter 11 - Laura Gilmore

https://www.flickr.com/photos/genbug/

Chapter 12 - Ritu Raj

https://www.flickr.com/photos/rituraj64/

Other Books By The Author

Product Management

- How Product Managers Can Sell More Of Their Product: Tips & Techniques For Product Managers To Better Understand How To Sell Their Product

- How Product Managers Can Sell More Of Their Product: Tips & Techniques For Product Managers To Better Understand How To Sell Their Product

- How To Create A Successful Product That Customers Will Want: Techniques For Product Managers To Boost Product Sales And Increase Customer Satisfaction

- What Product Managers Need To Know About World-Class Product Development: How Product Managers Can Create Successful Products

- How Product Managers Can Learn To Understand Their Customers: Techniques For Product Managers To Better Understand What Their Customers Really Want

- Product Management Secrets: Techniques For Product Managers To Boost Product Sales And Increase Customer Satisfaction

- Product Development Lessons For Product Managers: How Product Managers Can Create Successful Products

- Customer Lessons For Product Managers: Techniques For Product Managers To Better Understand What Their Customers Really Want

- Product Failure Lessons For Product Managers: Examples Of Products That Have Failed For Product Managers To Learn From

- Communication Skills For Product Managers: The Communication Skills That Product Managers Need To Know How To Use In Order To Have A Successful Product

- How To Have A Successful Product Manager Career: The Things That You Need To Be Doing TODAY In Order To Have A Successful Product Manager Career

- Product Manager Product Success: How to keep your product on track and make it become a success

Public Speaking

- Creating Speeches That Work: How To Create A Speech That Will Make Your Message Be Remembered Forever!

- How To Organize A Speech In Order To Make Your Point: How to put together a speech that will capture and hold your audience's attention

- Changing How You Speak To Overcome Your Fear Of Speaking: Change techniques that will transform a speech into a memorable event

- Delivering Excellence: How To Give Presentations That Make A Difference: Presentation techniques that will transform a speech into a memorable event

- Tools Speakers Need In Order To Give The Perfect Speech: What tools to use to create your next speech so that your message will be remembered forever!

- How To Create A Speech That Will Be Remembered

- Secrets To Organizing A Speech For Maximum Impact: How to put together a speech that will capture and hold your audience's attention

- How To Become A Better Speaker By Changing How You Speak: Change techniques that will transform a speech into a memorable event

- How To Give A Great Presentation: Presentation techniques that will transform a speech into a memorable event

- How To Rehearse In Order To Give The Perfect Speech: How to effectively rehearse your next speech to that your message be remembered forever!

- Secrets To Creating The Perfect Speech: How to create a speech that will make your message be remembered forever!

- Secrets To Organizing The Perfect Speech: How to organize the best speech of your life!

- Secrets To Planning The Perfect Speech: How to plan to give the best speech of your life

- How To Show What You Mean During A Presentation: How to use visual techniques to transform a speech into a memorable event

CIO Skills

- How CIOs Can Bring Business And IT Together: How CIOs Can Use Their Technical Skills To Help Their Company Solve Real-World Business Problems

- New IT Technology Issues Facing CIOs: How CIOs Can Stay On Top Of The Changes In The Technology That Powers The Company

- Keeping The Barbarians Out: How CIOs Can Secure Their Department and Company: Tips And Techniques For CIOs To Use In Order To Secure Both Their IT Department And Their Company

- What CIOs Need To Know In Order To Successfully Manage An IT Department: Decision Making Skills That Every CIO Needs To Have In Order To Be Able To Make The Right Choices

- Becoming A Powerful And Effective Leader: Tips And Techniques That IT Managers Can Use In Order To Develop Leadership Skills

- CIO Secrets For Growing Innovation: Tips And Techniques For CIOs To Use In Order To Make Innovation Happen In Their IT Department

- Your Success As A CIO Depends On How Well You Communicate: Tips And Techniques For CIOs To

Use In Order To Become Better Communicators

- What CIOs Need To Know About Working With Partners: Techniques For CIOs To Use In Order To Be Able To Successfully Work With Partners

- Critical CIO Management Skills: Decision Making Skills That Every CIO Needs To Have In Order To Be Able To Make The Right Choices

- How CIOs Can Make Innovation Happen: Tips And Techniques For CIOs To Use In Order To Make Innovation Happen In Their IT Department

- CIO Communication Skills Secrets: Tips And Techniques For CIOs To Use In Order To Become Better Communicators

- Managing Your CIO Career: Steps That CIOs Have To Take In Order To Have A Long And Successful Career

- CIO Business Skills: How CIOs can work effectively with the rest of the company!

IT Manager Skills

- How IT Managers Can Use New Technology To Meet Today's IT Challenges: Technologies That IT

Managers Can Use In Order to Make Their Teams
More Productive

- How To Build High Performance IT Teams: Tips
  And Techniques That IT Managers Can Use In Order
  To Develop Productive Teams

- Save Yourself, Save Your Job – How To Manage
  Your IT Career: Secrets That IT Managers Can Use
  In Order To Have A Successful Career

- Growing Your CIO Career: How CIOs Can Work
  With The Entire Company In Order To Be Successful

- How IT Managers Can Make Innovation Happen:
  Tips And Techniques For IT Managers To Use In
  Order To Make Innovation Happen In Their Teams

- Staffing Skills IT Managers Must Have: Tips And
  Techniques That IT Managers Can Use In Order To
  Correctly Staff Their Teams

- Secrets Of Effective Leadership For IT Managers:
  Tips And Techniques That IT Managers Can Use In
  Order To Develop Leadership Skills

- IT Manager Career Secrets: Tips And Techniques
  That IT Managers Can Use In Order To Have A

Successful Career

- IT Manager Budgeting Skills: How IT Managers Can Request, Manage, Use, And Track Their Funding

- Secrets Of Managing Budgets: What IT Managers Need To Know In Order To Understand How Their Company Uses Money

Negotiating

- The Art Of Packaging A Negotiation: How To Develop The Skill Of Assembling Potential Trades In Order To Get The Best Possible Outcome

- Getting What You Want In A Negotiation By Learning How To Signal: How To Develop The Skill Of Effective Signaling In A Negotiation In Order To Get The Best Possible Outcome

- Exploring How To Get The Deal That You Want In A Negotiation: How To Develop The Skill Of Exploring What Is Possible In A Negotiation In Order To Reach The Best Possible Deal

- Use The Power Of Arguing To Win Your Next Negotiation: How To Develop The Skill Of Effective Arguing In A Negotiation In Order To Get The Best Possible Outcome

- Learn How To Signal In Your Next Negotiation: How To Develop The Skill Of Effective Signaling In A Negotiation In Order To Get The Best Possible Outcome

- Learn The Skill Of Exploring In A Negotiation: How To Develop The Skill Of Exploring What Is Possible In A Negotiation In Order To Reach The Best Possible Deal

- Learn How To Argue In Your Next Negotiation: How To Develop The Skill Of Effective Arguing In A Negotiation In Order To Get The Best Possible Outcome|

- How To Open Your Next Negotiation: How To Start A Negotiation In Order To Get The Best Possible Outcome

- Preparing For Your Next Negotiation: What You Need To Do BEFORE A Negotiation Starts In Order To Get The Best Possible Deal

- Learn How To Package Trades In Your Next Negotiation

- All Good Things Come To An End: How To Close A Negotiation - How To Develop The Skill Of Closing In Order To Get The Best Possible Outcome From A Negotiation

- Take No Prisoners In Your Next Negotiation: How To Start A Negotiation In Order To Get The Best Possible Outcome

Miscellaneous

- How To Heal A Broken Leg – Fast!: Understanding how to deal with a broken leg in order to start walking again quickly

- How Software Defined Networking (SDN) Is Going To Change Your World Forever: The Revolution In Network Design And How It Affects You

- The Power Of Virtualization: How It Affects Memory, Servers, and Storage: The Revolution In Creating Virtual Devices And How It Affects You

- The Internet-Enabled Successful School District Superintendent: How To Use The Internet To Boost

Parental Involvement In Your Schools

- Power Distribution Unit (PDU) Secrets: What Everyone Who Works In A Data Center Needs To Know!

- Making The Jump: How To Land Your Dream Job When You Get Out Of College!

- How To Use The Internet To Create Successful Students And Involved Parents

Techniques For Product Managers To Better Understand What Their Customers Really Want

This book has been written with one goal in mind – to show you how to find out what your customers really want from your product. We're going to show you how to listen to what your customers are really telling you.

Let's Make Your Product A Success!

<u>**What You'll Find Inside:**</u>

- **PRODUCT MANAGERS NEED TO KNOW HOW MUCH TIME TO INVEST IN A PROSPECT**

- **PRODUCT MANAGERS NEED TO UNDERSTAND HOW TO UPGRADE CUSTOMERS**

- **PRODUCT MANAGERS NEED TO LEARN TO K.I.S.S. THEIR CUSTOMERS**

- **PRODUCT MANAGERS NEED TO MAKE THE PRODUCT PURCHASE PROCESS PERFECT**

Dr. Jim Anderson brings his 4 college degrees coupled with over 25 years of real-world experience to this book. He's managed products at some of the world's largest firms as well as at start-ups. He's going to show you what you need to do in order to make your career a success!

www.ingramcontent.com/pod-product-compliance
Lightning Source LLC
Chambersburg PA
CBHW071754170526
45167CB00003B/1030